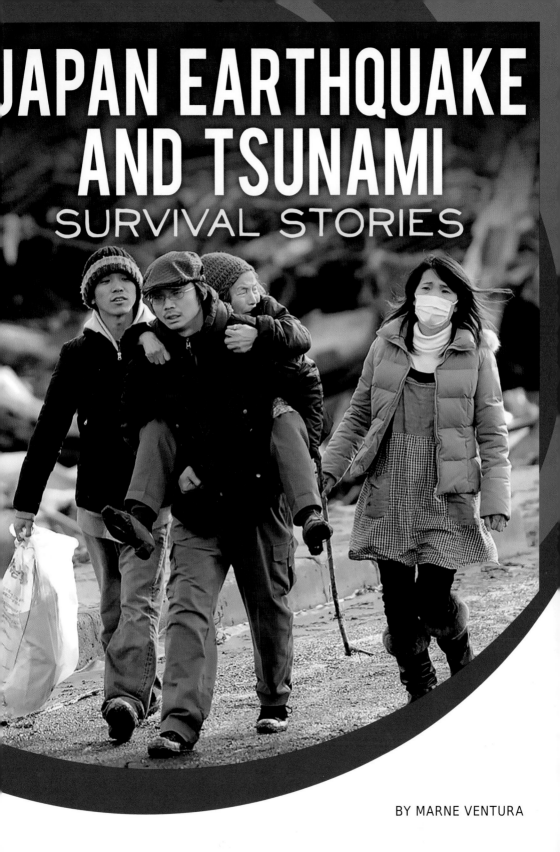

JAPAN EARTHQUAKE AND TSUNAMI
SURVIVAL STORIES

BY MARNE VENTURA

Published by The Child's World®
1980 Lookout Drive • Mankato, MN 56003-1705
800-599-READ • www.childsworld.com

Acknowledgments
The Child's World®: Mary Berendes, Publishing Director
Red Line Editorial: Design, editorial direction, and production
Photographs ©: Kyodo News/AP Images, cover, 1; Yasushi Nagao/The Yomiuri
Shimbun/AP Images, 6; Ho/Reuters/Corbis, 9, 10; Dorling Kindersley/Thinkstock,
11; The Yomiuri Shimbun/AP Images, 12, 24; Masanobu Nakatsukasa/The Yomiuri
Shimbun/AP Images, 14; Red Line Editorial, 15; Kyodo/Newscom, 16, 18, 26; Yomiuri/
Reuters/Corbis, 20; TK, 21; iStockphoto, 22; Kimimasa Mayama/EPA/Corbis, 28;
Jonathan Woodcock/iStockphoto, 29

ISBN 9781634074254

LCCN 2015946314

Printed in the United States of America
Mankato, MN
December, 2015
PA02288

ABOUT THE AUTHOR

Marne Ventura is the author of 24 books for kids. She loves writing about
nature, science, technology, health, and crafts. She is a former elementary
school teacher, and she holds a master's degree in education. Marne lives
with her husband on the central coast of California, where she survived the
San Simeon earthquake in 2003.

TABLE OF
CONTENTS

DISASTER STRIKES

March 11, 2011, began as a pleasant Friday in Japan. On the northeast coast of the island of Honshu, in the city of Sendai, business people were going about their days. Outside the city, rice farms and fishing ports bustled with activity.

Just before 3:00 p.m., the ground rumbled. Buildings swayed. At first, most residents were not too worried. Earthquakes often occur in this area. Many homes and offices in Japan are made to withstand shaking. But people quickly sensed this quake was different. The movement continued for six minutes. Furniture moved, windows broke, and ceiling tiles fell. Fires broke out. Roads buckled and bridges broke.

Twelve minutes after the quake, officials sent out a tsunami alert. Tsunamis are big waves that are caused by earthquakes in the ocean. But in the confusion that followed the big quake, many people in Japan did not have time to get safely to high ground. In less than one hour, waves as tall as 128 feet (39 m) swept onto the coast. People able to find safety on the tops of tall buildings watched as the rushing water lifted houses, cars, and ships as if they were toys.

In the days after the tsunami, the death count rose. Thousands of people were missing. Waves that traveled across the ocean were still almost 8 feet (2 m) high when they reached Alaska and Hawaii. **Debris** from the damage in Japan washed ashore in the mainland United States and Canada.

FAST FACTS

Size
- **Magnitude** 9.0

Location
- **Epicenter** on ocean floor, 45 miles (72 km) east of Tōhoku, 15 miles (24 km) below surface

Damage
- 15,853 people killed, 6,023 injured, thousands more never found
- Total of 1.1 million buildings damaged or destroyed, including 6,751 schools and more than 300 hospitals

Chapter 1

ADRIFT AT SEA

At the time of the earthquake, 60-year-old Hiromitsu Shinkawa was at work in a lumberyard. After the ground stopped shaking, he rushed home to check on his wife, Yuko, and pack some things. Shinkawa heard a tsunami was coming. He thought he could get the things he wanted and wait safely on the upper floor of his home when the waves hit.

Shinkawa did not know the size and strength of the approaching tsunami. When he and his wife reached the second floor of his house, a wave crashed through the house's windows. Everything went black. He thrashed, frightened, beneath the water. Kicking and paddling, he was able to get his head above the surface. He looked around, desperate to find something to help him stay afloat.

The roof of his house had been torn off and was floating nearby. He swam toward it through the cold water. When he got

◀ **A tsunami approaches houses northeast of Tokyo on March 11, 2011.**

close, he tried to pull himself onto a section of broken roof. He slipped off three times. On the fourth try, he was able to stay on. Where was Yuko? Shinkawa saw no trace of her. In the **turbulent** water, he could only hold on and wait for help.

As the sky darkened, Shinkawa heard the knocking of debris in the water around him. All night, he clung to the roof fragment, cold and alone. When the sun rose, he could see he had washed far out to sea.

Shinkawa felt a surge of hope at the sound of helicopters in the air. He tried his best to stand up on the wobbly roof to signal for help. But six aircraft passed without noticing him. In the distance, he saw land. He tried to sit up and paddle. But the water was churning so much he had to lie flat to keep from tipping over.

By the end of the day, Shinkawa was **dehydrated** from lack of food and water. His skin was white from exposure to saltwater. He was cold and miserable. It was another long, chilly night. All he could think about was how much he missed his family.

When the sky lit up on the second morning, Shinkawa found that the ocean had washed him closer to land. He searched the floating debris but found nothing to eat or drink. Helicopters again flew over. Again, they did not come to him. When a warship passed without seeing him, he began to lose hope.

▲ Shinkawa signals for help from the floating roof of his house.

But Shinkawa did not give up. He **salvaged** a scrap of red fabric and a pole from the ocean and made a flag. When the warship passed his way again, he held on to his raft with one hand and waved the flag with the other. A light flashed from the ship. The crew had seen him. He was filled with relief as the ship approached.

▲ Rescuers bring Shinkawa (center) aboard their ship after picking him up miles away from the coast.

Crew members pulled Shinkawa on board and gave him a drink. He gulped the liquid down and burst into tears. "I thought today was the last day of my life," he told his rescuers.[1]

Shinkawa was taken to a hospital and found to be in good condition. Rescuers had discovered him nearly 10 miles (16 km) off the coast. He had drifted for 43 hours. He was reunited with his daughter and grandson. But his wife, Yuko, had been swept away by the tsunami. She had not survived.

HOW AN EARTHQUAKE CAUSES A TSUNAMI

Sometimes, two plates of the earth's crust push against each other on the ocean floor. When they slip or break apart, energy is released that shakes the ground. The ocean water above the earthquake becomes displaced. This causes a tsunami.

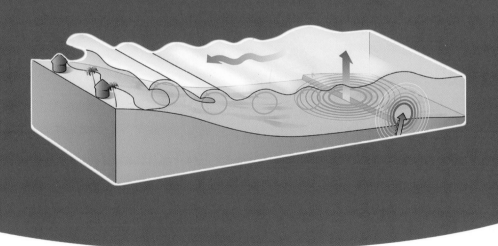

Chapter 2

THE IMPORTANT THINGS IN LIFE

On the afternoon of March 11, 2011, Ayumi Osuga was playing with her three children, who were between the ages of two and six. The 24-year-old factory worker was doing origami, the Japanese art of folding paper, inside her single-story home in Sendai, Japan. Suddenly, the ground began to shake. Dishes fell from the cupboards and broke on the floor. Osuga was not too concerned. Earthquakes were part of life in Sendai.

Then, she heard her husband yell, "Get out of there now!"[2] The tone of his voice told her that she and the children were in danger. She quickly gathered them up and rushed outside. She and her husband got everyone into the car. If a tsunami were coming, they needed to get to high ground as fast as possible. There was no time to worry about the house or anything in it.

◄ People in cities near Japan's coast had less than an hour to get to safety after the earthquake.

▲ Survivors walk through debris-filled streets in Sendai one day after the tsunami.

Osuga's relatives owned a home on a hilltop 12 miles (19 km) away. The tsunami waves moved as fast as jumbo jet. But Osuga and her family were able to make it to safety. Once at the hilltop home, they settled in for the night. It was cold and dark. The hills around them still had snow on the ground. Osuga lit candles and listened to the radio for news about the tsunami.

On Sunday morning, she and her husband drove back down the hill. She needed to find out what happened to her home. She wanted to make sure her neighbors were okay. Tears filled her eyes when they arrived. Except for three large packs of diapers, her home and all her belongings were ruined. Everything was soaked in dirty water.

As she sifted through wet papers and photos, a team of firefighters arrived. They were there because two of Osuga's neighbors had died in the tsunami. Osuga was shocked to hear her neighbors did not make it to safety. It made her even more grateful that her husband and children were safe.

TSUNAMIS AND LANDMARKS

This graph shows the height of different landmarks compared with the heights of some of the tallest recorded tsunamis in history. The 2011 Japan tsunami was the tallest since 1964.

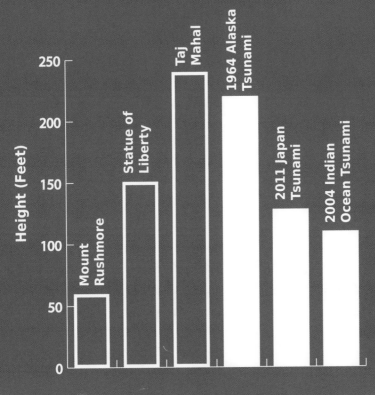

Chapter 3

SWIMMING FOR HER TEAM

On the afternoon of March 11, 2011, 16-year-old Chihiro Kanno and her friend Mami Sannomiya ate lunch together as they always did. The two were students at Takata High School in Rikuzentakata, Japan.

After lunch, they left the school to go to swim practice. The swimming center was located near the seaside in Rikuzentakata. The girls changed into their swimsuits in the center's locker room. As they were getting ready to go to the pool, the earthquake struck. The swim-team members knew they were supposed to go to a local community center if there was an emergency. Chihiro rushed to put on her school uniform over her swimsuit. She was upset and frightened by the earthquake. She could not stop crying during the drive to the emergency shelter. Mami held her hand and tried to calm her down.

◀ **High school students from Rikuzentakata walk to class on August 17, 2011.**

At the shelter, an official directed the girls to the second floor. He told them a tsunami was coming. Chihiro ran up the stairs, holding tight to Mami's hand. When they reached the landing, another official told them to go to the third floor. That's when the tsunami hit. Water flooded into the building. Chihiro gripped Mami's hand as the wave lifted her up, but the choppy water pulled Mami away.

Chihiro was sucked down by the water. Her body flipped twice, and she hit the floor. She could not get herself up to the surface. She thrashed her arms and kicked her legs. Finally, her head popped out of the water and hit the ceiling. Treading water, she had barely enough space to hold her face out of the water.

She heard people around her, but it was too dark to see. She called out and a teammate answered. The girls held hands as they treaded water. Slowly, the water receded. Chihiro's feet once again touched the floor as the water emptied out of the room.

Chihiro was trapped inside the building with 11 other survivors for the entire night. **Rubble** filled the stairs and corridors so they could not get out. Broken windows let cold wind flow through the building. Chihiro had lost her shoes and could not feel her feet. She was cold, wet, and terrified.

◄ **Whirlpools can develop after tsunamis strike. Whirlpools pull in water and debris from the surrounding area.**

▲ **Helicopters were important for reaching stranded survivors after the tsunami.**

A helicopter arrived in the morning. Rescuers helped the survivors out of the building. They took Chihiro to a shelter. She stayed there for three days before her parents found her. They thought she had not survived. Chihiro learned that her friend Mami and six more of her teammates died in the tsunami.

Six months after the earthquake and tsunami, Chihiro and her family were living in a small temporary home in Rikuzentakata. Despite her frightening experience, she still wanted to be a part of her swim team. "I want to swim my best for my teammates who lost their lives," she said.[3]

CHIHIRO'S LOCATION

Rikuzentakata was hit hard by the 2011 disaster. Before the tsunami hit the city, many houses and buildings crumbled from the intense earthquake.

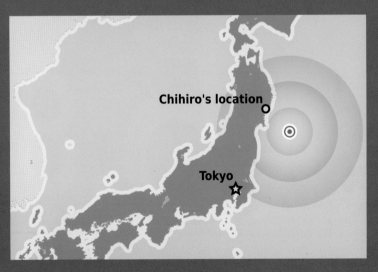

津波注意
Be careful of tsunamis

ここの地盤は

海抜 **5.8m**
Height above sea level

鎌倉市

Chapter 4

THE LONGEST DAY

Zack Branham grew up in Indiana in the United States, where earthquakes and tsunamis happen only in movies. The 24-year-old had travelled to the port town of Kuji, Japan, to teach English to young Japanese students. He did not speak Japanese, so he was lonely and homesick. Then, he met Georgia Robinson, an English teacher from New Zealand. When the two became close friends, Branham began to enjoy living in Japan.

On the afternoon of March 11, 2011, Branham was in his office in Kuji when the floor began to shake. The wheels on his office chair rolled this way and that. Supplies and books flew off shelves. Branham ran outside and was directed to go to the top floor of the city hall building.

Branham was able to get inside the city hall building and up to the top floor before the tsunami hit. He stood at the window and watched in amazement. The river below suddenly changed

◀ Japan is known for being prepared for tsunamis. But experts did not anticipate the strength of the 2011 disaster.

direction, receding. It turned from blue to dark and murky. Then, it moved back toward land, flooding everything in its path. Branham watched in panic. If the tsunami were this bad in Kuji, it would be worse in Noda, Japan. Robinson worked in Noda, about 8 miles (13 km) away, on the coast.

Branham tried to contact Robinson, but phone and internet services did not work. He decided to try to get to Noda. The water from the tsunami had receded enough for Branham to get into his car for the 15-minute drive. But the road to Noda was clogged with debris, rubble, and mud. Fires from downed power lines burned all around. Police officers stopped Branham and told him to go back to Kuji. With his limited Japanese, Branham understood only the word *dangerous* in their warnings.

Branham returned to Kuji and tried again and again to contact Robinson, with no success. By 5:30 in the morning, he was desperate to know whether she was okay. He got into his car again and drove toward Noda. He had to stop when the road was blocked by Japanese army troops. He pulled over and got out of his car.

Branham noticed groups of local people were walking into Noda with shovels. They were volunteers, helping to clean up. Branham pulled the hood of his sweatshirt over his head and

◀ **The 2011 tsunami easily washed away vehicles and buildings throughout northeast Japan.**

slipped into the line of workers. He was able to walk around the police officers and soldiers and enter the small town.

Branham was shocked by the devastation in Noda. Half the town was gone. Debris was everywhere. Fires burned all around. Would he find Robinson? Was she safe?

First, he went to her apartment, which was at the top of a hill. It was still intact, but no one was there. From the hill, Branham could see down to Robinson's office in town. It was in ruins. He hurried to the kindergarten where she sometimes taught, but it was also destroyed. Next, he went to the junior high school where she usually worked. A handful of teachers were there, but they had not seen Robinson. They suggested he try the elementary school.

He went to the elementary school, but the teachers there had not seen Robinson either. Branham was losing hope. He was exhausted, cold, wet, and hungry. As he was leaving, a van pulled up. Branham recognized two of the men in the van. They were Japanese employees at the board of education. Branham could not ask them for help in Japanese, so he showed them Robinson's photograph and business card. They seemed to know where she was.

◀ **A member of the Japanese military helps evacuate residents from Noda.**

▲ **Aid workers and volunteers from around the world came to help Japanese communities struck by the 2011 earthquake and tsunami.**

The men motioned for Branham to get into the van. They drove him to a building downtown. The two men went inside and told Branham to wait in the van. Suddenly, Robinson came out. The building was the headquarters for Robinson's teaching program. She had been in the building the whole time. Branham rushed toward her and gave her a hug. It had been an exhausting 24 hours since the earthquake.

Branham stayed in Kuji to help clean up after the disaster. He knew he was fortunate to be a survivor. He wanted to help the people of northeast Japan recover.

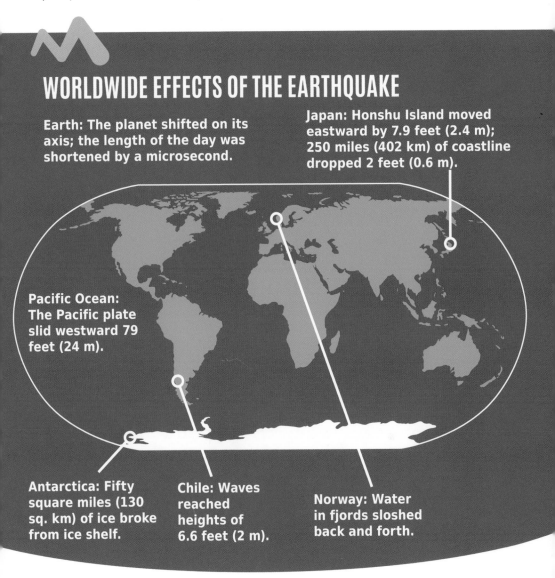

WORLDWIDE EFFECTS OF THE EARTHQUAKE

Earth: The planet shifted on its axis; the length of the day was shortened by a microsecond.

Japan: Honshu Island moved eastward by 7.9 feet (2.4 m); 250 miles (402 km) of coastline dropped 2 feet (0.6 m).

Pacific Ocean: The Pacific plate slid westward 79 feet (24 m).

Antarctica: Fifty square miles (130 sq. km) of ice broke from ice shelf.

Chile: Waves reached heights of 6.6 feet (2 m).

Norway: Water in fjords sloshed back and forth.

GLOSSARY

debris (duh-BREE): Debris contains pieces of wreckage or broken things. The streets of Sendai were filled with debris after the earthquake.

dehydrated (dee-HYE-dray-tid): Someone who is dehydrated suffers from a lack of water. People who didn't have drinking water after the tsunami became dehydrated.

epicenter (EP-i-sen-tur): The place on the earth's surface above the starting point of an earthquake is the epicenter. The epicenter of the 2011 Japan Earthquake was in the ocean, off the east coast of Honshu Island.

magnitude (MAG-ni-tood): Magnitude is a measurement of the size of an earthquake. The magnitude of the 2011 Japan earthquake was measured at 9.0.

rubble (RUHB-uhl): Rubble is the concrete, bricks, and stones from a broken building. Ayumi Osuga's home was reduced to rubble by the earthquake.

salvage (SAL-vij): To salvage is to pull and use something from the ruins of a disaster. Hiromitsu was able to salvage materials from the ocean to make a flag.

turbulent (TUR-byuh-luhnt): When something is turbulent, it is moving roughly or violently. Debris from the damage caused by the tsunami knocked about in the turbulent water.

SOURCE NOTES

1. Julian Ryall. "Japan Earthquake and Tsunami: The Man Who Floated Out to Sea on His House Remembers the Tragedy." *The Telegraph*. Telegraph Media Group Limited, 2 Mar. 2012. Web. 29 Jun. 2015.

2. Associated Press. "Disaster Survivors Recall Moments of Terror." *Fox News*. FOX News Network, LLC, 14 Mar. 2011. Web. 29 Jun. 2015.

3. Damian Grammaticas. "Six Months On: Japan Tsunami Survivor's Story." *BBC.com* British Broadcasting Corporation, 12 Sep. 2011. Web. 29 Jun. 2015.

TO LEARN MORE

Books

Mara, Wil. *Why Do Earthquakes Happen?* Tarrytown, NY: Cavendish Square Publishing, 2010.

Tarshis, Lauren. *I Survived the Japanese Tsunami, 2011.* New York: Scholastic, 2013.

Wendorff, Anne. *Tsunamis.* Minneapolis, MN: Bellwether Media, 2013.

Web Sites

Visit our Web site for links about the Japan earthquake and tsunami: childsworld.com/links

Note to Parents, Teachers, and Librarians: We routinely verify our Web links to make sure they are safe and active sites. So encourage your readers to check them out!

INDEX